THE MAKING OF

THE MAKING OF CASABLANCA

Shelah Florey

HEARING EYE

Acknowledgments

'Before the Planes Landed' was previously published in *Camden Voices 24;* 'The Other End of a Dive' and 'Mouthpiece' were published in *Envoi;* 'Appreciated Later' and 'Royal Machines' were published in *Morley New Writing 4.*

With many thanks to Dinah Livingstone for her warm encouragement and practical help.

Published by
Hearing Eye
Box 1
99 Torriano Avenue
London NW5 2RX
Copyright © Shelah Florey 1999
ISBN 1 870841 60 3

Cover design copyright © Emily Johns 1999

This publication has been made possible with the financial assistance of the London Arts Board.

Contents

Highgate Cemetery East 1
Slim Cycling 2
Not Intended 3
Dispatch 4
Windsor in November 5
Appreciated Later 6
Continuing the Tradition 7
But Where People are Involved 8
A Pause at the Ballot Box 9
9.96 Seconds that were Different 10
A Bandage with Faith in the Future 12
Holding a Camera at the Time 13
At the Flats — Evening 14
Somewhere Else in the Building 15
The Road Indoors 16
On Returning to the Room 17
Anti-Moonlight 18
True Life Stories in the Library 19
On the Heath — In Memoriam 20
That Can't be Visited 21
The Improvement 22
Right — Well That's It for the Time Being 23
I'd Forgotten 24
Stamping Ground 25
A Move before April 26
Let's Go to the Park 27
Scenario for a New Baby 28
Passing the Primary School 29
A Picture of Madame Monet and Child 30
To Be With 31
Becoming a Sister 32
The Last of It 33
Hitting Another Shore 34
Coming at it Sideways 35
The Sea on Hold 36
At the Edge of a Pond 37
The Other End of a Dive 38
Come and Sit Down this Breezy Day 39

Diving Upwards 40
No Mistaking their Aridity 41
Flute 42
Athlete in a Concert Hall 43
The Repetition of a Phrase has been
    Continuing for Some While 44
Old Time Dancing at the Festival Hall 45
A River that Got Through 46
Pay Attention and You May Hear It 47
Early Tunes 48
They're Not the Same as Violins 49
Between One Thing and Another 51
Anxiety with Wings and Legs 52
Mouthpiece 53
Royal Machines 54
Out of their Hands 55
Special Appearance by Courtesy of Chamois 57
Myth of the Morning 58
Before the Planes Landed 59
Upon a Time 60
The Making of Casablanca 61

HIGHGATE CEMETERY EAST

Apart from the angels and the trees
what I notice here
is the massive head of Marx
all brain and idea —
caught in bronze
twelve feet above the earth.
No wings of course —
he's not going anywhere.

Though they may have thought
of him as once —
those desperate people
from all lands —
if not leading them to heaven
at least away from hell.

SLIM CYCLING

Once it knew
the body could never forget,
could poise like an acrobat
and always come back to this place.

Find where it was —
in this street
among the juggernauts and cars,
the huge noise —
a centre. Thin.

With just enough there
to pass between engines
with some kind of grace —
skimming a fine line,
taking the risk.

NOT INTENDED

It's supposed to be for walking on —
for going somewhere
to keep passing strangers.
It's the wrong place for the people
who need to stay here
and lie still.

Dreams are for bed
(if they're managing to sleep at all).
Their mussed hair, just visible,
is too conspicuous for us —
their bodies closely wrapped in blankets
still spread
like accusations on a pavement
we meant for other reasons to be hard.

DISPATCH

She sells evening papers —
it's a job, she's been doing it for years.
What you don't expect
are the song and dance routines,
the one woman party,
the knees-up at people passing in the street.

She's old of course and probably drinks.
But still — I think it's attitude
she's high on —
the no importance to her
of events, world-shattering — whatever,
that she shoves unfolded into other hands —
with a hectic unconcern
is glad to get shot of every evening.

WINDSOR IN NOVEMBER

It was clean though,
it was honest
it came out into the open
of its own accord —
I knew what it was doing
straight-away.

I had this castle
on fire
said the Queen
and went to it at once —
for a while I could
look as sad in public

as I'd felt all along.
It was wet outside
by then.
I wore my boots,
took off the crown —
put a rain hat on.

1992.

APPRECIATED LATER

This was a time
when clapping at funerals began —
not just in an Abbey
but as the coffin was passing by.
I was startled —
it was a sound you usually hear
at the end of a concert
or to cheer a parade.

Applause from the mourners —
it seemed no-one had told them,
lining the streets they did what they wanted —
were impulsive and different.
I was startled at first
but then I could see what they meant.

Princess Diana's Funeral, 6th September 1997.

CONTINUING THE TRADITION

It was a spirits-were-not-dampened
-by-the-weather parade
as it often is in England.

The Guards moved in a square —
a tablecloth across the ground
which seemed to be just clearing up

from older banquets,
when the climate
wasn't all that different:

bringing in the colour red
to look a bit more cheerful.
Scarlet of course

not quite the same as blood.

BUT WHERE PEOPLE ARE INVOLVED

A building that's purposely blown up
because it's not needed any more,
or in the way,
can often sag quite gracefully —
still contained
sit down like a lady.
Taking a last deep breath,
it gives a low curtsey
to the camera.
You could say it's having a good death.

Oh, it's handled well —
so much better than countries
exploded from within —
their people having to leave home
and scattered on the dirt road
far beyond the town.

1994

A PAUSE AT THE BALLOT BOX

The moment was too precious
not to be held on to
and let it have its picture taken.

Too special
just to be slipped away quickly.
So it stayed suspended in his hand —

a time full of everything
he had to say.
Overcoming battles — arrest —

the island years
where he remained unheard.
An instant savoured

before he let it go:
he was free to join
all the other exiled voices

and come home.

Nelson Mandela voting in South Africa 1994.

9.96 SECONDS THAT WERE DIFFERENT

His eyes fastened
on the place where winning was —
it wouldn't get away this time.

He threw straight at it
all the years put in —
the extra strength he had

for overcoming not quite
reaching there before.
Till suddenly it started

towards him —
it couldn't resist a look
of such intensity —

knew where it belonged now.
Began to accelerate
so fast it almost took

his breath away —
and at last
lay under his feet

completely still.
The others found
an ordinary white line

that had kept
its distance
until it was too late.

Linford Christie winning the 100 metres, Olympics 1992.

A BANDAGE WITH FAITH IN THE FUTURE

There's a small bandage on his hand
carefully wound
round one or two fingers and a thumb,
as he holds his arm up to show
how he put his life-jacket on.

It looks at home
and sensible after the storm —
all that crowding in — the sea
with a huge indifference
as though he wasn't anybody.

This naturally assumes
he's going on. Accompanies him.
For being saved
it's what he has a right to now —
lifted from the waves alive.

It has a minder job to do.
Stays only as near as it has to —
taking care.
Waiting for his days to come —
for healing. The new skin.

A survivor from the Estonia. Sank 1994.

HOLDING A CAMERA AT THE TIME

The next moment she was swept away
into the falls.
She hadn't got off the rocks —
done anything to prevent it
but had stood there smiling,
taking pictures
ready to look at again
when she got home
and show to other people.

Perhaps she was skilful,
a good photographer
but she could only focus on the present —
see through the viewfinder
what was there now —
the high arc of the water, the white wonder.
The next second was too far.

From a news report.

AT THE FLATS — EVENING

I walk cement stairs
that are blotted with damp.
In fading light
a bird slips past the window.

My way runs up
between closed doors
where families lurk —
children grow quietly
in their beds
like mushrooms in the dark.

SOMEWHERE ELSE IN THE BUILDING

They seemed to live
operatically —
no mundane job to go to.
Where did they get
all the long arguments —
the great battles on the stairs.

Sex was it?
Love she was sure —
who went out with who
was a whore — a bastard
and let the other down.

It sounded almost epic
sometimes. As though
they were living the true life —
the singing one — the one
actually against the bone.

While she turned pages,
pressed buttons
and was reasonably
getting nowhere near
what it was really all about.

THE ROAD INDOORS

Heavy music travels through the flats.
Pounds on. Long distance.

It seems to be going somewhere
that it never reaches.

On either side a kind of life
is waiting, impossible to think about;

the drivers are insistent.
Can't stop, can't look, can't step down

to that alien land out there:
people talking to one another

ON RETURNING TO THE ROOM

The trouble was visiting at night
when normally I'd be asleep,
it was taken too much by surprise
and already somewhere on its own,
a place I wasn't needed in —

things that were scattered on the floor
had joined each other there.
The book — still open — that I'd come
back for was interrupted by the light,
caught hovering in territory

it couldn't leave immediately —
my hand invading as I took it from
the chair — pages half lifted in the air.

ANTI-MOONLIGHT

I see it as it is —
not how it's done or why.
As something on a roof
and not effective as a light.
I see it prowling for no reason —
it puts no life in plants
and as a heat appliance
I'd say it's less than useless.

It has its moments I suppose —
pulling waves around,
giving the burglar something to think about.
But all in all I feel
it's wasting valuable time
coming through the window.
I've already put that cupboard in the dark,
that ordinary chair;

I don't want some pale replica standing there —
that hologram,
half with me, half away somewhere.

TRUE LIFE STORIES IN THE LIBRARY

A chair clears its throat
as somebody gets up.
Computers pip —
people at the tables
skilfully ignore each other
two inches away.

There's a quiver
from the book I'm looking at
(first published 1955).
Pages swirl indignantly —
after all this time
now you want to talk!

The people sit between
their covers — an old man
no-one's read perhaps
for thirty years. A student
not quite sure what she's about yet —
referring . . . referring.

ON THE HEATH — IN MEMORIAM

The names printed on the seats are very still,
they won't be going where they once belonged
to that person moving in a room.
They have to stay with other people now
near water —
kites flying on a hill.

THAT CAN'T BE VISITED

A town down there
at the edge of the Heath
stretches out
in the late afternoon sun.
You can see the other end
with hills beyond —

sets of houses
and shining tower blocks
that don't make a sound.
But try having
a closer look —
it's stranger than you think.

Go nearer
it'll disappear —
something else is there
that's lost its shape,
buildings jostle
in the street —

all the silence
has gone out of it . . .
below here
is another city —
a place that can't be visited
not even once —

at the first approaching step
begins to draw
further into the distance.

THE IMPROVEMENT

At first they remind me of barbed wire
high against the background of the sky

but the air is good,
the wind is bringing something better

than it has been doing.
Along the line of branches the sharp bits

seem to notice and comply —
getting a softer movement in.

They're not so dark now — more green . . .
sounds like they're whispering.

RIGHT — WELL THAT'S IT
FOR THE TIME BEING

The trees on the hill are just sketched in
with here and there a dash of green
at random —
an inkling of what the whole thing's
going to look like I suppose
when it's properly worked on.

Though it seems a shame
just for the sake of spring
it has to lose
casualness —
the leaving it to us
to picture how the rest goes,
or like it as it is.

I'D FORGOTTEN

So what's all this then —
what's the hurry with the birds
the business in and out of trees
gratuitous whistling. Enterprise.

I'm the only one
who seems to have a problem here.
Bemused. With winter eyes
still coming in from somewhere else.

A novice really
while the leaves already swing
in their professional way. At my feet
insects just get on with it.

STAMPING GROUND

The trees gallop along the horizon
in a line. Up and down
past the church steeple,
the power transmitter,
the row of mock Tudor houses,
towards the Heath.

You can see them there
in groups,
shifting about on the hill —
the ones who've already made it
away from the streets.
Or just near the pond,
dipping down to the water.

A MOVE BEFORE APRIL

Some geese flew past
with a noise
of furniture being shifted,
their wings creaking
and substantial.

When I looked up
the line was unwavering —
they were at the end
of something tugging them.
A new place in the North.

LET'S GO TO THE PARK

Children are the trying again —
the hope of getting it right
this time,
down the road
clutching your hand —
beginnings in small clothes.

A prospect you take out
on sunny days
or a hidden face
in winter
under a hood.
You go slower than you used to,

well — growth needs to be
that long.
Halfway on the path
a looking up at you —
uncertain.

SCENARIO FOR A NEW BABY

At the beginning
it's allowed the usual noises
is into a language
of crying at the moment.

The round body isn't expected
to be doing very much —
gets by with the occasional
movement of the eyes —

sometimes a hand enquiring
about the corner of a cot —
and what is that
leaning over me . . .

questions accumulate
increasingly have the power
to pull out closed limbs
uncurl the arms and legs.

The earth has it all
worked out — won't leave
them lying very long —
into its caves and mountains

draws a daughter and son.

PASSING THE PRIMARY SCHOOL

They've gone home by now
but the window's open wide enough
for me to see their paintings on the wall.
The ones young children do —
first images of Mum and Dad.

I don't think they've spent hours
over these. They're being spontaneous here
and there's a kind of mastery.
They haven't learnt to fill
the details in yet —

the light and shade.
They need time. But then perhaps
the more skilful they become
taking care — putting in everything —
the more they may lose

that decision in the one-line-only mouth
hair flaring as though from a sun —
arms stuck open.

A PICTURE OF MADAME MONET AND CHILD

I don't want to question this too much.
They don't.
They've decided this is the best thing to do.
For no special reason.

Why shouldn't they be sitting in the garden.
She's brought her sewing
and the little girl a book.
There's a toy horse standing by.

It didn't need to be thought about a lot.
It's a fine day.
They've come out to spend time
near the hedge with all the flowers in.

Anyway, I like to think the artist
caught them here
fortuitously. If he didn't,
he gives us this idea.

TO BE WITH

A boy gets out in the afternoon
with a ball and kicks it around
in the area — he's by himself for a while.
It shouts against the wall —
goes off at a tangent

and argues with him in the grass.
With no-one else —
houses with their backs to him,
blank windows —
he's glad it does.

BECOMING A SISTER

A little girl
holding on
to the push-chair
steadily keeps pace —
already outside
of what she was.

Though in the mirror
when her mother
combs her hair
she sees no difference,
she understands
there must be.

Solemnly takes up
her altered place
in that small procession —
going to the shops
is another thing
she's getting used to.

THE LAST OF IT

Nobody came out
now it was October —
the ice-cream van
waited under the trees.

Until just one —
a child in her anorak
ran across the road
and reached up for the sun.

Unwrapped the bright colours
she'd known on longer days
when summer was there —
always — like a habit.

When others jostled her
and they went down
to the pond and swam,
in spite of all the notices.

It was forgiven then
it was all allowed —
going out to play
late in the evening.

Now the day
already ushers her indoors . . .
under the trees
the van starts up again —

accelerates away.

HITTING ANOTHER SHORE

On a winter afternoon
the water trails
on to a beach
that looked much the same
a year ago.

In the summer
people visited and left.

The stones stare out —
the sands are emptier
than if no-one
had ever been there.
The waves brought in

all the weeks between
and left them
unclaimed at the edge.
They continue doing
what they have to do.

Also the rocks and cliffs
are there many times over,
repeating themselves each day —
meeting the air
again and again.

COMING AT IT SIDEWAYS

The sea with a more obvious strategy today
lines up disconcertingly
in long ranks — and approaches.
At other times
I've seen it in the sun
just playing around
apparently,
toying, trinketing in smart-best-looking
-girly-skipping waves.
though somehow
it still manages to get
where it rubs itself against enormous cliffs,
taking off a few centimetres more.

THE SEA ON HOLD

Domestic as a tablecloth
the sea settles down
before the houses.

Earlier it was a creature
barely contained,
its claws reaching out
for the feet of small children.

It was difficult to tell
if the gulls
clinging to its back
were victims or there

for the ride.
Now they're in charge,
strutting in line beside
the soft, cotton-pale water.

Here and there
one or two folds appearing.

AT THE EDGE OF A POND

The trees form a semi-circle
as though they're about to dance.
The floor of water's green
and glittering from the sun.

When are they going to start . . .
no, I don't think they need
to move any further —
they're doing all right.

THE OTHER END OF A DIVE

The water was taken by surprise
and shouted out —
it issued a quick all-round statement:

Let me just say one thing —
you're breaking and entering
you really forced me into doing this!!!

Exclamation marks were everywhere
and a bright spontaneity
hung a little in the air.

But that was merely
camouflage — disruptive —
hiding a truer self

that somewhere further down
coolly closed ranks again
with a senior boom.

COME AND SIT DOWN THIS BREEZY DAY

The way the pond stops at the edges
is particularly well done. By then
the trees are welcome and the banks to sit on.

The water is travelling north and north
it's a direction not a place —
the grass is being that for all its worth.

DIVING UPWARDS

A fish is swimming in the sky,
only it's dry.
And it isn't actually
a fish —

it's the right colour — grey
(silver in the sun).
the sky's right too
only upside down.

NO MISTAKING THEIR ARIDITY

Deserts are always drying their hands —
give them a little water
and they use it up in no time.
They're eager to hold bright flowers
for a while — till the wind blows.

They prefer to be empty again
except for snake lines crossing —
scorpions trickling through their fingers.

FLUTE

Pushing a bright pin
into the air
the flute has
an immediate say —
making a hollow there
and filling it.

Never completely
part of the orchestra
or ever really in the hall,
it sets off
like a bird. Where —
beyond the houses

and recent cities —
there's space around
for songs that are better
on their own.

ATHLETE IN THE CONCERT HALL

The voice is standing still
on a single note
and preparing to spring
as high as it can go.

With a one-two on the spot
it gathers impetus
and sets out
on further little steps

approaching the scary height
of a top C . . .
soars above it —
hovering a minute

giving itself airs.

THE REPETITION OF A PHRASE HAS BEEN CONTINUING FOR SOME WHILE

Living in a sunny house
for a long time —
the clocks are working well,
every morning
it's fine —
the weather never changes.

Curtains stir
as they did yesterday.
a tune's
beginning —
goes on
the same way.

Others join in
and play —
they like to be together,
stay
in harmony.
Six pianos.

Barbican Piano Festival.

OLD-TIME DANCING
AT THE FESTIVAL HALL

It was the nearest thing
to an indoor sea
people slowly waltzing.

Grey/white heads freely
against all
the landlocked things nearby —

table and chair
pillars
with their one idea.

A RIVER THAT GOT THROUGH

It was just the one hall
but there was no surprise
that in this space
the music flowed so far —

that in spite of walls
and attendants on the door
the pianist went on rowing
a good hour.

PAY ATTENTION AND YOU MAY HEAR IT

The house and darkness outside
should meet each other head-on
without being separated
by anything between.
Turn the stereo off . . .

listen — don't you notice something —
that collision in slow motion
with the sound down.
That's how things should
really play at night.

It's there already — written out.
All you have to do
is lift your fingers from the music
for a while.
Because the beats are silent

it doesn't mean there's nothing going on.

EARLY TUNES

I don't notice so much whistling now,
people have personal stereos they listen to
and walk with down the street.
Birds stick to it of course but they still
use trees. They're always in the old days.

Though occasionally it's a sound I hear
coming from a garden shed or kitchen,
where someone's working with their hands —
as though they're small wings
they still find useful.

THEY'RE NOT THE SAME AS VIOLINS

Using the civilised
throat of a cello
to say what they think
they say: she's very collectable
or she's not what I had in mind.

Or he has a face
like a good quality chair —
French probably
Parisian to be more exact.
He doesn't go out much.

(Why are men in Paris
so much more indoor
than anybody else
even when they're standing
on the pavement.)

Coming back to the low-toned
string instrument —
its voice is fine
if you don't want to have
hysterics over anybody

make a fool of yourself
or put forward
some impulsive proposition
that simply won't do
in the circumstances.

It has a sound
that listens to itself
but that doesn't mean to say
it's without passion —
it catches fire slowly.

Cello people
fall in love
in their own sort of way.
And when they do
it goes very deep.

BETWEEN ONE THING AND ANOTHER

A neck is an erotic zone
also a despotic one.

People who stick theirs out
are asking for it —
it's not too difficult to hit
or get two hands round
really tight.

Then again you might
get stuck on one a different way —
have just your eyes fastened
on the bare
perfect run of skin
from the bottom of the hair.

An engineer would say
it's a cable-laying place
to where your thoughts are
and your face —
if he's just the engineer
that is.

ANXIETY WITH WINGS AND LEGS

It can enter through a gap
you didn't know was there,

with a small buzz saw
get to work around your head —

follow you from room to room.
You try giving it more space —

well surely it can feel the air
sense the whole world of freedom . . .

it clings.
Stab stab with its tiny legs

as though there's no way out.
Strange — it was so clever once

making an entrance.
What's the matter with it?

MOUTHPIECE

The woman was talking to her dog.
She spoke to him in sentences
quite long and involved.

Unfortunately he'd never been
to school. No-one had taught him
very much English
even as a foreign language.

Anyway it wasn't necessary —
he stood patiently,
naturally polite
letting her get on with it.

Why keep a person and talk yourself.

ROYAL MACHINES

Just before they go in a gate
or leave the room
I've noticed people bending
down a little
with a look towards —
from a small distance
putting the car alarm on,
the video on pause.

And I wonder
could this slight obeisance
be the beginning
of a lot more homage to the machine.

OUT OF THEIR HANDS

I never seem to meet
just a person lately,
they're always trailing
a machine round with them.

It's become so dominant
I feel I ought to greet it first.

Say good morning to the Walkman,
the revving car,
the hedge cutters loud enough
to be demolishing a house.

I shouldn't be surprised
if they answer back quite soon.

Uncivilly of course:
Shut your face,
bugger off —
who said it was a good morning.

Well, I don't blame them really
they must be up to here

with those feeble appendages
hanging on to them.
They want to find themselves,
get out into the world

set up on their own —
be independent.

And the way it's going
it won't be long before they are —
ready to switch off anyone
getting in their way.

SPECIAL APPEARANCE
BY COURTESY OF CHAMOIS

The man who does the windows
clambers up a ladder
and pushes against the glass.

He comes in closer contact with the clouds
than I ever can.
Making them so clean
his face is in them.

MYTH OF THE MORNING

The taxi beats
outside the house
in the early morning.

A passenger
steps down alone —
and at this hour

separately from everyone
it doesn't seem
the usual transaction

but an older
kind of relationship
of rider and carrier

when vehicles
were creatures sometimes
journeys a quest

and the return at last.

So the traveller
bends towards it
handing out his gold.

BEFORE THE PLANES LANDED

Once there was a far place
distant and separate
living within itself
keeping its secret.

Special clothes — first dances
few saw only
after long expectations
and a wild journey.

Entirely new hills
birds in pristine skies
a strange set of the land,
ingenuous eyes.

UPON A TIME

Since they learnt it was possible
to blow the whole world up
in one go

they liked their songs
and stories
to be open ended.

It was different before,
they could finish them off
quite neatly

without looking over their shoulder.

THE MAKING OF CASABLANCA

They didn't know
how the film was going to end —
the actors came in every day
to a script that wasn't finished yet.
Who was going to get the girl
and who . . . it was very difficult.

They never imagined it would be a classic.

Why not. Perhaps the actors
were convincing because they didn't know,
like we don't —
every day a new bit of the script.
And it's the wondering comes over

in Casablanca. The love puzzle.
The not-until.
They got to the end finally of course —
the characters in their different ways.
Like we will.